C'e ... T
mine recently wrote
this book and I
found the messages in
it ones I wished I
had learned years ago.
May you find encourage-
ment through her words.

HINDSIGHT Love,

LESSONS LEARNED BPuter

THE HARD WAY

Kathleen Tysinger

cover photography by
Grace Tysinger

For Grace:

The person- Grace, my beautiful daughter, and the process- grace, being gifted with what you don't deserve.

One in the same.

Contents

16. You don't have to agree to be agreeable.

17. Most friendships in high school, however close, are a blip on the radar.

18. Family comes in many forms.

19. Reciprocal relationships.

20. Don't settle.

21. Choose love.

22. Hurting people hurt people.

23. Don't expect people to be other than who they are.

24. If you've blown it, own it.

25. Cheer others on.

26. Not everyone will like you.

27. You will never be able to please everyone. Ever.

28. The freedom of saying "no."

29. Be open-handed and generous.

30. Choose quality over quantity.

31. Don't expect someone to read your mind.

32. Don't assume you know how someone else feels.

33. It's not all about you.

34. Motives.

35. Don't judge where you haven't walked.

36. In closing.

Foreword

This is written by an imperfect woman with a sincere desire to save you, my sweet girl, from the tears, the hours, the years I spent on these things, these fallacies, these issues.

These are the lessons I'd wish I'd understood much earlier in life.

The philosopher and writer, George Santanaya, once said "Those who do not remember the past are doomed to repeat it." This has often been paraphrased (which I prefer): "Those who don't learn from history are doomed to repeat it." While it's not your history, I invite you into the mess of mine and what I've learned from it.

The things that weigh on my heart, a mom's heart, that I pour out here are from hard-won experience, not a place of perfection or telling you how to live your life. They're from a girl who was, once upon a time, much as you are. One who sat across a kitchen table from someone older and wiser who could say things to me I might not listen to or receive from my own sweet mom, just because of where I was in my life.

These were women spoke volumes into me over a cup of coffee or tea. Not preaching to me, not criticizing me, but just sharing what life had taught them. So I pause to thank Terez Matkins, Susie Free, Jan Jacobson, and Norma Comer for their patience, their love, and their wisdom.

I realize you will inevitably make some of your own mistakes and learn your own lessons, but my heart is to give you a glimpse into things you can work around. The words in this book are broken pieces of brilliance borrowed from a thousand sources, and my hope is that this may help you live life fully.

Hindsight: A definition.

One dictionary defines hindsight as "recognition of the realities, possibilities, or requirements of a situation, event, decision, etc., after its occurrence."

Another definition reads: "Perception of the significance and nature of events after they have occurred." I think I like that one better. Seeing the importance of what is behind you more clearly than you could have seen it when you were in the thick of it.

The cover art for this book, shot by my own beautiful daughter, is significant. Looking in the rear view will accomplish *some* things, but not everything. If you only look at your rear view mirror, you'll see where you were, what's behind you, but you won't see what's coming right at you.

If you only look at your windshield, however, you miss crucial information that comes from what is behind you. Both are important for driving, but even more important for living. So, then, how do we choose our focus?

Here's the thing: the windshield is so much bigger than the rear view mirror. That's where your focus should be. That's where your energy should go: looking ahead and preparing for what's in the front view.

But that doesn't mean you never learn from what's behind you. You see things behind you from a different angle, with a different point of view from the perspective you had as they were looming in the future, barreling down life's highway toward you. This different angle, this different point of view, this information can help you as you make the decisions that lie ahead.

Glance in the rear view, look to what you can learn, and gaze through the windshield, ready for what life will bring.

YOU

1.   You are enough.

If you don't read past this entry, please just read this one. This is one of the most important things I've learned, and learned it the hard way. If I could right now, I would take your beautiful face in my hands, gaze unflinching into your wide eyes and say these three words: You. Are. Enough.

Smart enough, pretty enough, strong enough, brave enough, talented enough, worthwhile enough, just enough. You will hear (and have already heard) a million messages, a million lies from society and from those who would seek less than the best for your life, blurbs telling you that you need to be more, do more, have more.

I certainly did. And I bought it. And I spent my time, spent myself, striving to meet an imagined standard. An impossible standard. I felt over and over again that I was not enough. The voices inside me weren't satisfied, so I kept pushing. It took me years to uncover this lie, but such an incredible freedom comes when you get there. Know the inherent value you have, rest in the strength you already possess.

As you are right in this moment you are unspeakably valuable. You are precious beyond words. And you have everything you need to make a forever-imprint on this world. Custom made for this time and place. You are enough.

2.   Your decisions and choices matter.

I am the result of a rebound hook-up in a time when such a thing was not done, not accepted, and barely talked about. I was not planned, but was the result of a decision regretted later on.

I tell you this to illustrate an important lesson: You never know what your decisions are going to produce down the line. I am so grateful that, all those years ago, a terrified but courageous teenage girl, who I now know and love, had the selflessness and strength to give me to my wonderful family who had been waiting and praying for a baby girl for many years. Her decisions, both good and, well, "heat of the moment," gave me a wonderful life.

The decisions you make today and every day WILL affect your future, one way or another, for good or ill. Even the bad ones (and I've made many) can be redeemed to become blessings. I am living proof.

You are blessed with the freedom to choose in this one wonderful life you're given, but that doesn't mean you have freedom from the consequences of your choices. One choice leads to a consequence, which leads to another choice, then another consequence and so on.

It reminds me of a fender bender I saw the other morning. Three cars were lined up at a signal waiting for a green light, when the driver of the third car back jumped the gun, rear-ending the car in front of it, which was then shoved into the next car in front of it. Your choices can do the same thing, setting off a chain reaction, affecting others and your future before you're even out of the gate.

Consequences aren't exclusively negative; they can be positive as well. For example, the consequence of studying for a test is doing well on said test and eventually getting a good grade in the class. The consequence for getting up and working out or eating well is a healthier body. The consequence of being a good steward of your money is financial stability. The consequence for not doing those things is the opposite.

The choices you make in your teens and 20's will matter for the rest of your life. What do you want your life to look like? Think through the direction you're choosing. Ask yourself whether this trajectory will take you to the way, the path, the life you really want. Decide what habits to build into yourself, and start them now.

As your days go, so goes your life. If you want to reach certain goals, start building things into every day that lead you in that direction.

Success is never accidental. Ever. It's a long path. Think about your choices in light of the most likely consequences. Adjust accordingly.

3. Being is more important than doing.

Who you are will matter all your life. What you do is temporary.

So often we define and describe ourselves based on what we do: I am a student, I am a teacher, I am a business major, I am a stay-at-home mom, I am a (fill in the blank). However, when you define yourself only by what you do, and you can't do that thing anymore, what's left? Who are you?

I have struggled so much with this since I became ill and stopped doing most of the things that had defined me for years. I suddenly had no answer when people asked me, "And what do you do?" During the early phases of my illness, my kids, if asked what their mom does, would have said that I pretty much watch Netflix, knit, and occasionally cook. And they weren't wrong. But I'm not just what I do.

Look to your core, the center of who you ARE, not what you do, and decide what kind of person you want to be as you move through life.

"Being" has much more to do with how you relate to the people around you than the activities or work in which you engage.

Be who you are meant to be. Not a task list. Rather than solely defining yourself by your activity, by what you DO, think about defining yourself based on your characteristics, your core values, your character: I am compassionate, I am thoughtful, I am kind, I am passionate about (fill in the blank).

Again, you have a CHOICE about the kind of person you want to be. Look at the people around you who you most admire. Look at their character, not just their activity. Look at their attitudes. That is who they are.

Decide what you want to DO, what you do for a living, but more importantly, what kind of person you want to BE, the life you want to live.

4.   Create margins in your life.

Think of a piece of binder paper. Do you write on every square inch? From the very top edge to the very bottom, all around the punched-out binder ring holes, edge to edge? Of course not. That would be really hard to do, impossible to read, and it is totally unnecessary.

Now think of your life as that piece of binder paper. Sadly, I have been tempted most of my life to fill every square centimeter of my "binder paper" with something. My tendency is to plan and schedule every second of every day (and the world will see how productive I am!! Not.), leaving zero white space, not a tiny patch of breathing room to be seen. But just like a piece of binder paper covered completely, it makes for a mess and is hard to decipher. And it's totally unnecessary.

So what happens when something unexpected needs to be written into life? And by the way there's always something unexpected, not of your own planning, screeching in unannounced from left field. Where can it fit if my page is already covered completely? It has no where to go, no bandwidth left to deal with the unexpected. That's where I lose it. If every possible space on my binder paper of life is completely covered I simply can't handle one more thing.

Life is filled with the unexpected, which is why living with some margins is so vital for your own sanity. Create some white space in your schedule to just be still. To read, or grab a nap, or take a hot bath.

I soldiered on for years proving (to nobody at all) that I needed no down time. But I desperately did. That doesn't make someone weak. It makes them human. Taking care of yourself isn't selfish, it's wise. And no one notices if you're being a martyr and taking everything on, by the way, so knock it off. No one else is going to say, 'hey, you're taking on too much, don't do that." You know your own limits. Respect them. You can't make any tea if there's nothing in the pot.

You have to find the balance for yourself and know where those margins are. Put them in place. Mark them. Guard them. It's worth it.

5. It doesn't have to be Paris- find the beauty in everyday.

I am dying to go to Paris one day. And one day I will.

I love the idea of the Eiffel Tower, the history, the rivers, the museums, baguettes and strong coffee, perhaps even a striped tee, skinny jeans and a jaunty beret. But it's not where I live.

I love the idea of soaking in the culture, listening to the beauty of the language spoken with such smooth sophistication. And the food. But I'm not there. I'm here.

And while enjoy the dream, I love my own reality. Even when it's not perfect (and it never is, never will be, by the way).

I have learned that finding the beauty and the gifts in the "normal" is one of the greatest teachers of gratitude. My mom is queen of this. I remember as a kid and teenager, every spring she would point things out to me: the blossoms, the yellow wildflowers covering the pastures, the

California poppies blooming unbidden by the side of the road, the new grass making our golden hills green again, the baby animals in the fields we drove by. I (being a kid/teen) rolled my eyes at the time. But she was so right.

Finding the beauty in every day is one of the keys to being content. It changed my perspective completely, looking at the world deliberately and with gratitude, finding the gifts that are everywhere.

Love what you have in front of you and see it clearly. Pause to admire the clean lines of a pure white mug, steamy with coffee on a winter morning. Take a few moments of silence and breathe in morning air. Revel in sunshine on your face. Appreciate blossoms on the trees in front of Target (or wherever) every February. Snuggle into that blanket on the couch. Relax in how awesome bed feels at the end of a long day. Or warm fresh-from-the-dryer clothes. Or the first night on clean crisp sheets. The slant of sunlight coming through your bedroom window. The laughter of those you love. Beauty and gifts are all around you.

Notice. Pause. Be grateful.

Life is hard. But life is also beautiful. Choose to see that; be intentional. Paris is a dream. But your life is what is happening here and now. Don't miss it.

"Life is what happens to you while you're busy making other plans." -John Lennon

6. Spend yourself on what matters

It is so easy to fill every waking moment with things that don't matter. Even though you're young and you have a million years ahead of you (or so it seems now), time will fly by you and your life is the sum of how you spend your days.

Don't get caught (and I'm telling myself this as much as you) in the loop of mindlessly scrolling through life, distracted from the people around you by the trivialities, the phone in your hand, social media.

This is so much easier said than done. There are a thousand things that vie for your attention. Constantly. And there is a great temptation to go on autopilot, to spin your wheels, and to just go through the motions.

But you can make an impact EVERY DAY. Look for the opportunities and take them. Even if it's just taking an extra moment with a friend, a family member, a stranger, to really see them. Or pausing to just be still and listen, just take some quiet un-plugged time. Decide what matters most. Do that.

7. Let it go.

Not just an overplayed song from Frozen, but sound life advice. Don't be one to hold a grudge. Move. On. Be the first one to apologize, be the first one to forgive, truly forgive, and be the first one to move past.

Does that mean you have to fully trust someone who has legitimately lost your trust? No, it does not. I love this quote by William Paul Young: "Forgiveness is not about forgiving, it is about letting go of another person's throat." You may still need to use caution in a relationship, but be the first one to extend grace.

Forgiving truly is a gift you give yourself as much as one you give the offender. You choose to lay down a burden that can crush your soul and, thus, move forward in your life. Does it always mean verbalizing your forgiveness to the offender? Nope. Sometimes that is neither possible nor practical to do that. Forgiving must, at times, be a process in your own heart and mind, having little to do with the other person.

I have struggled through this experience personally. I was sexually assaulted in college, as so many young women are, and carried the emotional scars of this horrific experience for many years. I would grow anxious every year as the anniversary of the assault came around, would struggle with nightmares, would feel the weight of this long-ago event afresh every year.

After 15 years I finally came to a place where I had to forgive my assailant for this horrible offense. He didn't ask me to. I hadn't spoken to him in, well, 15 years. But for my own sake, for my own heart, for my own health, I had to move past and truly forgive him. I did it for myself. Having received so much grace in my life, how could I not extend it to someone else?

So I chose. Chose to mourn and move past, and chose then (and forever more) to let go of his throat. It was NOT easy, but it felt like a weight was lifted from my heart, truly. I no longer felt defined by this trauma, no longer dreaded the anniversary of this event, and, in time, no longer gave him a second thought.

Another 5 years passed and I was led very clearly by the Spirit to do something very out of character for me. I was led to Google this guy's name. Scary. So I did. He's. A. Pastor. I kid you not. I prayed about WHAT in the world I was supposed to do with that. And I heard loud and clear: Forgive him. I responded, yeah, well, I've already done that. Loud and clear: But he doesn't know that. Ah. So, I did something else scary, and emailed him. At his church.

I had to take a bit of perverse glee in the moment of terror that my initial email must have elicited when he saw it, but I basically told him that I had forgiven him years ago for what happened on that warm September night in 1988, and I really felt like he needed to know that.

Well. He was floored. He shared that he had spent so many years burdened by what he had done, feeling the guilt and shame of it, and feeling unworthy to speak God's Word at all. And now he felt as if a weight had been lifted. He was truly, deeply, sorry, and being the father of a daughter and the husband of a wife, he could clearly see how profoundly he must have hurt me.

I didn't wait to have him ask me for forgiveness; that never would have come. I chose to forgive and extended grace. These were some of the hardest things I've had to do, to truly forgive to let it go, but choosing this path gave me the freedom to move forward unencumbered.

Choose to let it go. Give yourself the gift.

8.   Love yourself.

Be comfortable in your own skin. It's easy to say, really, but not such a simple thing.

I recently watched a video in which people of all ages and both genders were asked one question on camera: "What would you change about your body?" The answers of adults were very specific. One woman hated her forehead. She'd been teased by other people, had this feature referred to as a "five-head," and it was all she saw when she looked in the mirror. One man wished for smaller ears; he'd been called Dumbo a lot as a kid. One woman wanted to be taller, one wanted smaller thighs, one man wanted a less rounded/chubby face. They all identified physical "flaws" they wanted to change.

Then the video showed children who were asked the same question. One little girl wanted fairy wings so she could fly. One wanted a mermaid tail. One boy wanted shark teeth so he could eat bigger bites of food. One sweet girl said she wouldn't change a thing, she liked her body just the way it was. Wow. When is it, exactly, that we shift so drastically and so detrimentally from one view of ourselves to the other?

To be transparent, this was (and still is) so hard for me, just loving and accepting myself as I am. My whole life I saw all the girls (and later, women) who surrounded me as being more than I was: more attractive, more fashionable, more possessing of that perfect body type that I would never ever have. Ugh. There are so many times in my life that, if asked that same question on the video, I would have replied that I wanted to be 10 (or 20) pounds lighter, wanted smaller hips/thighs, wanted my skin to clear up, wanted my hair to cooperate more, wanted to be more athletic, etc.

But time and circumstances change one's perspective. More recently I would have said that I wanted my body to be free of my shiny new chronic illness, wanted the pain to go away, to feel strong and healthy again, to have my abundant levels of energy back. Different, yes, but still registering a level of dissatisfaction with what I am.

Honestly, here's the secret to a perfect body:

You already have it. You are a unique and beautiful person and you were custom made with the perfect body. Perfect for you and for what you need to do. You are designed to be who you are, authentic and true, not a cheap imitation of someone else.

So be you. And embrace it. Does that mean you never work hard to be healthy, be your best, do your best? Not at all. But make it YOUR best, not someone else's.

All of your uniqueness is what makes you precious and special, these differences are things that are custom designed, deliberate, and can be used to strengthen and grow you, to position you for your life's work. Whether it's thicker thighs (ahem) or a chronic illness, these things don't detract from who you are, they are PART of who you are.

Chances are the things you hate about yourself aren't things people see in you, they're things you see in yourself. As I observed the people in the video I referenced before, I saw NONE of the flaws that burdened them, the things they wanted so much to change. I saw beautiful people. We truly are our own worst critics.

Perfection is an illusion at best and a toxic lie at the worst. Don't fall into that trap; you are so much better than that! Be you. And be your own kind of beautiful.

Remember back to the days you were comfortable being you and choose to fly again with those fairy wings.

9.   Treat yourself like you would treat your best friend.

As women we are very, very hard on ourselves. We criticize what we see in the mirror, the numbers that show up on the scale, our performances, our perceived failures, every detail of every part of ourselves. We jump all over things we see in ourselves that we would NEVER criticize in our best friend. We would just think she's great. And we would love her because of who she is, the whole package, not one tiny event or element of her.

Why is it, then, so hard for us to extend the same grace, the same kindness to ourselves?   If you're going through a hard time, carrying a lot of stress, saddened by a situation, show yourself the same compassion you would show someone you love. Would you tell your best friend to get over herself? No! Would you immediately hand her a pint of Ben & Jerry's? Or would you listen to her, hug her, be willing to just be with her? Encourage her? Bring her flowers or a bath bomb to pamper herself? Take her out for a pedicure?

Treat yourself kindly. Choose to show compassion to who you are now and who you are becoming. You know yourself better than anyone else, and you know your needs more than anyone else. Be good to yourself, see yourself through the same lens you use for your best friend. Then do for you what you would do for her.

10. Be hospitable to yourself.

If your most favorite person in the world was coming to visit (someone you know or someone you don't but you admire from afar), wouldn't you make sure things were prepared to welcome them, to make them feel special and honored, to pamper them?

Hours and hours of my life have been spent in a frenzied panic when we were expecting guests who were important to me. There was cleaning, hysterics during the cleaning, asking aloud why no one was helping me freak out/clean… But this was all in the name of making my guest feel welcome, treasured, loved, and special.

It occurred to me fairly recently that I should be hospitable not only to those visiting my home, but to those IN my home. I should think of how best to welcome myself (and my people) to our home. Our best shouldn't be reserved for infrequent visitors, it should be our norm in our own haven.

If you love a certain type of candles, don't save

them for guests alone, have one to enjoy in your own space. If you love a bubble bath with said candle, make sure you have some lovely bubbles around from time to time. If you love a certain brand of sparkling Italian mineral water, why wouldn't you keep a bottle in the fridge? Use the beautiful towels, the nice dishes, the pretty glasses. Make yourself happy.

Life, my dear girl, is a special occasion. Celebrate it daily. You are the most frequent guest in your home. Make yourself feel truly welcome.

11. Embrace the challenges.

Hard things will happen. Tough times will come. Challenging circumstances are inevitable. Don't be surprised- it's all part of life. You can't decide whether or not hard things will come, but you can choose your response. You can elect to see these difficulties for what they are, eyes wide open, and truly embrace them in your life, arms wide open.

It's these hard things, these things that push you beyond where you ever thought you could go, that will grow you and define you, that will strengthen you.

I look back on many such times in my life, when, instead of embracing the hard things, I fought and kicked against them, even when the difficult path was clearly unavoidable. This made the whole experience that much harder, and it most likely took longer.

Be more courageous than I was; seize the challenge and know you will have the strength to get through it!

12.   Seasons.

Nothing on this earth is truly "forever." The hardest of things and the best of things are with you only for a season. Even in relationships or situations that are ongoing, there are shifts- subtle though they may be- but changes nonetheless.

I can remember feeling like high school would never end. Then it did. Same thing with college, or even some specific classes. All I can remember thinking was that this was hard and it was never, ever going to be easier. But then it was over. I have felt like being alone/in a hard place in a relationship/in a painful spot personally would go on without end. But it didn't. The situation did change, and it was better. Or at least different.

This became even clearer to me as I've raised a family. Seemed like not sleeping through the night due to the delightful needs of a fussy baby would never, ever end. But it did. Seemed like potty training would never be done. But it was. Seemed like junior high years with my kids would never be finished. But they were.

On the flip side, there are seasons in my life I've mourned as I've had to let them go, seasons in my work life, seasons of friendship, seasons when my kids were small and filled with wonder...but they pass just like the hard ones, sometimes leaving a feeling of loss in their wake rather than a feeling of relief.

Here's the key to navigating all this: Just go with it. Embrace the change in seasons.

Consider how the seasons change during the year. When winter turns to spring, does it make sense to insist upon wearing your heaviest winter coat every day? When you're surrounded by your flip flop and t-shirt clad friends sitting outside, why would you swaddle yourself, sweating profusely, in a wool hat and ski jacket? And when the fall rains are pouring down, your shorts and sandals that were your constant companions all summer long are now out of place and don't keep you protected. They may have been perfect to keep you comfortable in the previous season, but are FAR from comfortable in the new season.

When we try to force something from another season into the one we're currently in, it will always feel awkward and out of place, even if it's something we really liked in the other season. For example, it feels out of sync and awkward to listen to Christmas carols while basking on my sun-drenched patio with iced tea in hand, even though I love Christmas carols.

When the seasons in our lives change, we have to be prepared to let go of (or at least put away for a while) the things that were particular with the old season that don't work for the new season. That can take SO many forms! It could be habits, or expectations, relationships, lifestyle choices, career or educational paths, priorities, opinions.

It is important to see each new season clearly, and look for what will work in that season. And honestly, each season has amazing, wonderful things about it, things that won't be replicated in any other time in your life.

Appreciate- truly embrace- each season for what is, glean from it, learn everything you can from

it, knowing change will come. It is inevitable.
And different can be good. Change can be
stressful, but it can grow you in ways you
wouldn't see if you were forever allowed to
remain static, right in your comfort zone.

In the novel of your life, a hard season isn't a
period, it's a comma. Or a semi-colon. There's
a lot more to come. It isn't over.

YOU +
EVERYONE
ELSE

13. Control

Vital, vital lesson that took me so many years to really get. I'm still struggling.

You can't control other people. Period. You can't make them be/do/think as you think they should. Even if they're YOUR people. Nope. They are individuals.

You can't control most circumstances. You simply have no say in how many things in the world work out, and said circumstances may affect you profoundly whether or not they were of your making. This is maddening.

You can't control people, you can't control circumstances in which you find yourself, BUT you can control how you respond to both. You have a choice. You are completely in control of your response to people and circumstances.

I like to control things, and I have learned in no uncertain terms that I can't. I used to really struggle with this, freak out when people's behavior or other things didn't match with the lovely picture I had in my head, but I'm learning more and more that the freak-out does little besides make me (and the people around me) miserable. Understanding what is beyond my control is a big step in my growth.

Choose well how to deal with the things you have within your control, release the things that aren't under your control, and keep eyes wide open to see the difference between the two.

14. Respond rather than react.

They sound similar, but they're not. Seriously.

Reacting rushes from your gut, from your emotions, from your pain or outrage, and is usually unfiltered. And usually regretted almost immediately.

Responding comes from your head; it means taking a beat, pausing long enough to really think through the situation, and formulating an appropriate way to deal with it.

I'm not suggesting you become an automaton who never has an emotional reaction- we're all flesh, blood, and (occasionally) emotional women- but taking that couple of minutes before you speak, before you send that text, before you post that status can make an enormous difference in your life and in your future.

I can attest to this lesson in my career, my friendships, my family, my marriage, and my relationships with my children. In the heat of the moment I have said or written things that I would give anything to retrieve, but alas, like an arrow shot from a bow, you can't retrieve what you said or make it as if you never said it.

This is really difficult, but can save you a world of pain in the long run. Just think. Then speak. Brain first, words second.

Sounds logical, but I know many who have yet to get a grasp on this concept and they live their lives doing damage control. Every time I have simply reacted without thinking through the potential weight of my words, just letting the emotion fly, there has been collateral damage. Sometimes irreparable.

I often get annoyed because I CAN'T think of a searing, witty retort when I'm upset, wishing I could eloquently put someone in their place. I usually think of the perfect comment for the situation at 3am. The day after the interaction when it would have been useful. While I occasionally fantasize about what it would feel like to come up with the perfect snarky response at the time, it's rarely a kind one, rarely values and improves the relationship, and would rarely be the best thing in the long run. Although it would feel good. I guess my tendency to be witty retroactively is a blessing in disguise.

You lose nothing by taking the time to ponder a response rather than blasting a reaction. And you can gain everything. A reasoned response will win you more respect, shield you from yourself (!), and allow you to reply using better perspective.

15.   Consider your audience.

When you're approaching any interaction, think about who you're talking to. Think about their background, your relationship with them, how open they may or may not be to what you're saying. Consider how what you're going to say will land with them and how best to present it. Keep in mind, too, that what you DON'T say is just as important as what you DO say.

Consider how you would talk to your best friend versus how you would talk to your interviewer if you're applying for a job. Or your manner and speech as you're presenting a project in a class as opposed to talking to your mom on the phone. In any case, choose your words carefully. And in a related topic…

Presentation is everything.
How you say something is equal to or greater than what you say. Honestly. You can say the right thing in the wrong way and completely blow a situation up. Think carefully about your words, your tone of voice, your body language, and your attitude. And while we're on the subject…

Timing is everything.
When you choose to have an important conversation can be just as crucial as the words and tone you choose.

If you know you're short on time, that's not the best moment to bring up a difficult topic. If you know the person you need to talk to isn't a morning (or night) person, don't choose that time for a deep conversation. If you know that person is struggling with something else unrelated to you (or is just in a bad mood for whatever reason), be sensitive to that and know that your discussion may not have the desired outcome, so you may want to delay it. If you see that person is in a very busy moment or seems really stressed, put your talk on hold for a more opportune time.

Communication is the lynch-pin of human relationships. Use it wisely. Become an expert at reading the situation or person and adjust accordingly.

16.   You don't have to agree to be agreeable.

There are as many opinions and outlooks in this wide wonderful world as there are people. My experience has taught that you can disagree fundamentally with someone, but you can still love them and respect them. And they, you.

If you only chose to love and bless the people who see the world exactly as you do, look like you, enjoy the same things as you, or have the same goals as you, that is a very short and limiting list.

You can learn so much from people who see the world through a different lens, different experience, different upbringing, different education, different culture. Don't miss out.

Someone who disagrees fundamentally with you could bring a richness to your life that would be missing if you've surrounded yourself solely with those who agree with you. People who love would you fiercely may see the world in a different way, but would stand with you through anything.

To quote my mother in law: if we were exactly the same one of us would be unnecessary."

Different does not equal bad. Be open to differences, embrace them, and learn from them. Look for common ground; it can be found in the most unexpected and unlikely of places.

17.   Most friendships from high school, however close, are a blip on the radar.

Most adults will agree with me wholeheartedly. I can't think of many people I know who spend ANY time with the people they knew in high school.   In general most high school friends drift apart very quickly after they go to their respective colleges.

I've gone to high school reunions and they're nice enough, but I find I have very little in common with the people I knew back in the day. I've found we don't need to interact a lot beyond Facebook.

You will make your lasting friendships in college and in the years beyond. Don't stress out over these high school relationships, who's popular, who's with whom, because they won't really affect your life in the long run.

Enjoy them, but don't let them define you. Appreciate knowing these people, but know that it's not a forever thing. For better or worse.

18. Family comes in many forms.

You will always have the family you're born into.
Appreciate them, love them, learn to embrace
the heritage that you come from. You won't be
exactly like the other members of your family.
You just won't. Because you're an individual
who is ready to spread her wings and find her
own way. And this is why children are born: to
become who they're meant to be.

Know, though, that your family is an important
anchor and constant. Not there to weigh you
down, but to give you roots and stability as
you're going forth into your amazing future.
They will love you beyond reason and without
borders.

Then there's the family you choose. This doesn't
replace or supersede your family of origin, but
you don't always end up living near family. The
family you choose can be part of your college
crowd, work friends, church friends, or other
friends, but these are people you know are just a
phone call away, ready to do anything you need.

This is so crucial. I am blessed with many people in this chosen family of mine. And they've often been the ones to support me when my family of origin couldn't. For example, my whole family was devastated when my dad died just a couple of days before Christmas. However, I knew all I had to do was send one text and my sister-by-choice, Dana, would be at my door that evening with the last minute items I hadn't yet picked up for Christmas. And a hug. And a lovely scarf. And a shoulder for me to cry on. And I would do the same for her in a heartbeat.

Family. It's sometimes by biology and sometimes by choice, but it's always bound by love. When pondering who these core people in your life truly are, consider this: who are the ones who would be (or already HAVE been) next to your hospital bed? Or would be visiting you someday in the nursing home? Those, my girl, are the ones to spend your time and your love on. Those are the ones who truly are your family.

19. Reciprocal Relationships.

Observation has show an overriding tendency in myself and women around me: we give a lot of ourselves to others. That being understood, it's hard to ensure that you're not the only one in a relationship who's doing all the giving. Difficult as this is, it is essential in any peer relationship, whether friendship or romantic.

As a teenager I was in a relationship with a guy who was, um, volatile. And I was always making concessions, working to keep him from being upset, arranging my life around his schedule and his moods, neglecting friendships because of him. And he took me for granted. 100%. This guy wasn't happy unless I was off-center and upset and he emotionally manipulated me to feel guilty if I wasn't meeting his every whim. Eventually, I broke up with him, which was hard since we went to the same small church and had the same activities in high school. I wasted a whole year of my life, one that I'll never get back, on this guy. But I learned some valuable lessons. You can't be the one doing all the giving and making all the concessions. It's not how a real relationship works.

Don't accept this counterfeit for love.

Look honestly at your friendships and relationships. There are times in almost any friendship where one or the other of you is "needy," but those times ebb and flow.

Sometimes you're the one who needs a shoulder to cry on, sometimes you're the shoulder. This is the essence of friendship, of relationships. It's healthy and it's vital to getting on in life.

But. You can't always be expected to be the supportive one who gives so much of herself, allowing the other person just take. That's not compassionate, that's unhealthy.

As an adult woman with kids I found myself in this type of friendship again, years after I thought I was past all that. This particular friend had gone through a rough patch right before I met her, and I was willing to be a listening ear and a supportive presence in her turmoil- and transition-filled life.

As time went on, it became evident she could

(and did) flip any conversation, even one in which I was baring my soul, to make it all about her. I further found when I needed support, she was not to be counted on. At all. She took, but didn't give. I tried talking to her about this (so scary), but she shut me down. It was, according to her, all my problem, not hers. So I "broke up" with her. Which was harder and more painful than I thought.

In any case, this concept of reciprocal relationships is so important. You are valuable enough to have relationships in which you are an equal partner. Your close relationships should involve people who are willing to put their own needs aside when you need something.

"We accept the love we think we deserve." A quote from Perks of Being a Wallflower. True, so very true. Remember that you deserve love- loyal, reciprocal, demonstrative love. Not dismissive, demanding, lopsided love that you have to placate or work for. Know the difference

20.   Don't settle.

Don't ever settle for a boyfriend (or eventually a husband) who <u>doesn't</u> sweep you off your feet and continue to romance you even if you've been together a long time. Period.

That doesn't mean flowers every day or spending a ton of money or writing love songs to sing over the loud speaker at a football game. It means someone who thinks of you, is a good student of who you are and what you love, who takes the time and makes an effort to show you in ways that are meaningful to YOU that you are the most important person in his life.

A man who truly values you will find ways to show it. It's making the effort and taking the time to think of you rather than himself that is the vital component here.

If he doesn't do this when you're dating, I can guarantee 100% he won't when you're married. You are worthy of being romanced and adored. Don't settle for less than that. You deserve it.

21. Choose love.

There will be so many times in your life when you have to choose your response to a conflict or disagreement in a relationship. Always choose love. Choose the relationship over proving something. Choose loving the person over being right.

I've observed this a thousand times in friendships, in my family (in all forms) and in my marriage, yet it took me so long to really grasp this.

I remember, years ago, befriending a young mom at church who just moved into the area. We spent time together on several occasions, her daughter playing with my youngest, just getting to know each other. Over coffee she revealed some issues she had, and rather than showing love and compassion, I proceeded to tell her how much she needed to fix this and how she should do it, barely stopping short of a step-by-step diagram and PowerPoint. Ugh. I physically cringe when I think of how horribly I handled this. It cost me the relationship, they elected to NOT return to our church, and I never saw her again.

Had I taken a beat, thought it through, and just gave her a listening ear and an understanding heart, she may have eventually asked me what I thought and I could have gently counseled her. Or not. Really, why did I think it was my job to "fix" her? But I took it upon myself to be "right" rather than choosing the relationship.

There is a time to speak the truth in love, but when you're all about proving your point, that's not the time. I've regretted that (and many other situations like it) so many times and wished I had the opportunity to go back and apologize. To choose love rather than being the admonishing authority.

There will be people in your life with whose decisions and views you disagree. Rather than trying to prove they're wrong, just choose to love them. Focusing on the relationship and showing love is often the costly path, but always the best path.

22. Hurting people hurt people.

I heard this phrase for the first time when I was substitute teaching in one of the district's, well, sketchier schools. I was subbing for middle schoolers and there were some particularly disrespectful and vocal kids under my care. They were blatantly rude, hurtful to their classmates, and didn't really seem to care if they got into trouble.

I talked to another teacher about a few kids in particular, and she shook her head. Those poor kids had horrible home lives, abuse, addiction or crime in their families, and no one really seemed to pay any attention to them. Hurting people hurt people, she told me, a saddened look on her face.

It is in times of great stress or pain that I'm most apt to lash out or retaliate. Something, anything to make me feel better or more in control. Not saying that makes sense or is remotely fair. Can you identify with this? This is not a logical thing at all, sometimes it's barely a conscious choice, but it happens to us all.

When someone is thoughtless, harsh, or just plain unpleasant to you, try to step back and see what pain might be below the surface. Give the grace, compassion, and benefit of the doubt they probably don't receive from many sources.

23.   Don't expect people to be other than who they are.

This sounds odd, I know, but let me explain.

My son is an introvert; I don't expect him to want to come to a large gathering of people he doesn't know well or to feel comfortable in social situations.

There are people in my world who share quite liberally all they know about someone else, so I don't expect them to keep a confidence or secret.

One friend has a track record of canceling plans at the last minute, so I'm not surprised or disappointed when she does.

Set your expectations of people based on your observations and their behavior rather than your wishes or desires.

Why do I make this point, you may ask? Well, I've watched someone (call them Party 1) repeatedly expect someone else (Party 2) to behave in ways inconsistent with their core character, against everything they've ever seen and known to be true about that person's behavior and tendencies. Party 1 then feels disappointment, anger or frustration because Party 2 did exactly what they always do. All this turmoil because of unrealistic expectations. People are going to be who they are.

This has caused huge rifts in many relationships. Does this mean I'm cynical and don't think people can change? Not at all. I have changed enormously over my years, but I have also learned to adjust expectations and love people for who they are instead of expecting them to be who I want them to be.

24. If you've blown it, own it.

I hate messing up. I hate making a mistake. I hate it when I hurt someone else. I REALLY hate it when someone is upset with me.

So in my past, ashamed as I am to admit it, I haven't always responded the best way when I'm in that situation. I have tried to lay blame at someone else's feet for my mistake. I've become defensive and angry (when I was in no way justified to feel that way) when I was the one who made the mistake. I have just wimped out and hidden instead of "manning up" and setting things right.

But as I've gotten older, I've learned that the best way to handle this, the fastest way to heal the problem, is to just own the part I had to play and apologize to the wronged party, whether confronted or not. Let me say that again: apologize even if they don't bring it up.

Be the bigger person. It's hard and it's humbling and it's scary, but please believe me, it's the right thing to do.

Nothing destroys relationships (whether personal or professional) like a lack of trust. If someone can't depend on you to own up to a mistake, how can they trust you?

Own your mistakes, learn from them, and move past them.

25. Cheer others on!

Someone else's success does not rob you of yours. In our competitive world, this is a hard concept to get on board with, but it's essential in building relationships.

I have, throughout my life, seen my peers achieve things I haven't achieved. Or be recognized in ways I wanted to be recognized. Or succeed in a field in which I want to succeed. This doesn't mean *I can't*.

This doesn't take my opportunity, because her success was HER opportunity. Mine just isn't here yet.

Be someone who supports and cheers on the people that surround you. Be the one who encourages others to do and be their best. It doesn't take anything away from your achievements and will bring people around you who will support and celebrate your successes with you.

Life is not a competition. Your friend's awesome grades or success in a competition or great vocal performance doesn't erase yours!

We need to choose encouragement and shine the spotlight on those around us. Your turn is coming.

25. Not everyone will like you.

Whether we want to admit it or not, this is true. No matter how hard you try, there are some people with whom you will simply not connect.

I spent a lot of my life desperately wanting everyone to like me and wanting anyone who didn't like me to let me know what I had done to make them not like me so I could immediately fix myself. Well, that didn't work so well.

Just as there are some people you will encounter to whom you are instinctively drawn, there will be some in life with whom you just don't feel that connection. So the same is true of people who aren't you.

Some personality types are naturally drawn together, some groups are brought together for common interests and goals, and some are just thrown together and end up getting along wonderfully (like me and my 2nd college roommate, Jennifer, the most unlikely match).

We all want acceptance and to be liked. It's basic human nature. But if you can learn this lesson and pour into those relationships that ARE a fit for you instead of trying to make everyone happy, it is vastly more rewarding than spending yourself on relationships that aren't right for you.

26.   You will never be able to please everyone. Ever.

This is a big one to embrace. I can't even begin to tell you the time I wasted trying to make all the people happy all the time.

No matter what path you choose, someone will always want it to be different, some will be very vocal in telling you what you should have done instead, and some people will just not talk to you.

This is NOT to say you shouldn't listen to wise advice from people you trust, people who may have more life experience, but you can't take into account every single person's happiness, comfort, or opinion when making decisions. Ultimately you have to do what is truly best for you and those for whom you are responsible.

I am a pleaser by nature, as are many women I know, but learning that you have to prioritize those who you try to please is a vital life skill, one that's taken me years to hone.

On a related note: There is just no pleasing some people. Ever.

Some people you encounter in your life will never be happy. And that's because they're choosing not to be happy.

Sadly, some people spend their time focusing on all the things that are wrong with their world and not on their blessings. Granted, they may have had some pretty hard things to get through in life. But many people remain trapped there, in a holding pattern of misery, because they don't make the choice to climb out of their pit.

Love them, be kind to them, but don't expect things to change. They will most likely not be pleased by most of what you offer them. You can't fix them.

27. The Freedom of "No,"

You don't have to say yes to everything you're invited (or requested, or demanded) to do. You get to choose. This is, again, an area I have struggled with most of my adult life, people-pleaser that I am. I wanted people to be happy with me, approve of me, or like me, so I took on tasks, requests, and burdens that simply weren't mine. And they overwhelmed me.

I began to get the gist of this whole "saying no" thing, at least in my personal life, when I went back to work full time several years ago. I could say no to things outside of work because I simply didn't have the time or energy (physical or emotional) to take on anything else and still have anything left for my family. This was not to say that I didn't take on ALL THE THINGS at work, because that's what happened. Not good. Overwhelmed at work quickly led to overwhelmed all over my messy life.

This past year has taught me even more, however, that there is a great freedom in "no." I HAVE TO say no to a lot of things, which makes me more selective about what I do take on, what invitations I do accept. And I've learned that people will still like me and value me even if I don't do all the things.

You aren't required spend everything you have of yourself on things that aren't yours to do. Don't say yes just to say yes. Not everything is your assignment, however good the thing may be.

Look carefully at the bigger picture of what you're already carrying, weigh whether this potential addition to your world will be good for your life, your heart, your relationships, your health, your spirit. If your answer is yes after you take a long hard look at the big picture, dive in. If it's no, be direct. But be gracious. "I appreciate you asking, but I'm afraid I can't commit to that right now," is my new favorite response.

28. Be open-handed and generous.

Life is full of blessings. Be ready to share them.

As you give of yourself, your time, your resources, your gifts and talents, you will end up being blessed. And I promise, living life with a generous heart, you will always have enough.

I try to go through my whole house at least once a year, sometimes twice, to find things I don't use (where do these things COME from???) to donate. If I haven't used/worn/enjoyed it in a year, it goes. There are a few small exceptions to this rule, a few special keepsakes I am not able to part with, but it's a great feeling to be able to pass on things to someone who could truly be blessed by them. And we still have plenty of things. More than plenty.

We were the recipients of generosity so many times when we were a young couple, from family, from friends, and from strangers. So I have always felt the urge to pass things on. Bless someone's life with something you don't need or want.

Even more challenging, bless someone with something you DO need or want! I've seen this lived out with many lovely people I know. A friend of mine gave away her Bible to a total stranger seated next to her on a cross-country flight. Her favorite Bible, one she had loved, written notes in, highlighted, and used for many years. And she handed it over to a woman she was sitting with, not because she didn't want it, but because this woman didn't have a Bible.

You never know how much a simple, small act of generosity can make a difference. Be willing to be the blessing.

29.   Choose quality over quantity.

I've discovered in my more recent years that this phrase is true in many arenas of my life. For a long time I thought "more is better" in pretty much every area. More friends. More clothes. More stuff in my house. But as I have walked further down the path of my life I have come to realize that "less is more."

I have discovered the value of a few friends, people who will be with you no matter what, is far greater than a roomful of people who most likely want something from you and will walk away in a heartbeat when things are hard. Or talk about you when you're not there. A few people who know my soul and with whom I can laugh, cry, and vent are worth a thousand superficial relationships or the illusion of being popular. Quality over quantity.

A few really great pieces of clothing that I love, that fit perfectly, and that are good quality, exactly my style, and express who I am are far superior to a closet stuffed with things from Forever 21 that are worn once. Or not worn at all because they go with zero things in my wardrobe. Just saying. You should be able to go to your closet and have at least one really great outfit that is perfect for almost any occasion. It doesn't have to cost a fortune, but it should make you feel like a million bucks. Edit what you have, wear what you love.

A few home accessories that have meaning as well as beauty are what make it our home, not just filling any empty space with the latest decorating trend. Don't amass things that aren't meaningful. Be ready to pass on what no longer serves your purposes. They're just things. And again, could bless someone else when they're passed on. Meaning over mass.

30. Don't expect someone to read your mind!

I shake my head and chuckle as I write this. One of my hardest lessons.

I ASSUMED many times as a young wife that my beloved would read my mind and know exactly what I was thinking or feeling, what I needed (physically or emotionally), and, as should any good husband, would immediate act accordingly without any prompting from me whatsoever. Imagine my shock, annoyance, and disappointment when he could not actually look into my brain or heart and discern what was going on in that internal circus of mine. And I would get mad at him for not doing that. I have not always been the mature (ha!) and rational (ha ha!) person I am now.

I had to learn the hard way that I actually needed to communicate what I wanted or needed. And the vast majority of the time, when I communicated that want or need he was more than happy to help me.

This isn't just a man/woman thing. It's a basic human interaction thing. Be sure to communicate clearly with your family, your roommates, your friends, workmates, whomever, what you need, what you want, and what's on your mind if you have any hope of working through things.

Those conversations are crucial for setting up realistic expectations and following through with things that are important in any of those relationships. You can do it in a great and loving way, but do take the time to talk. Unless your people have telepathic properties that my people have somehow missed out on. And if they have said powers, don't tell me, I'd just be jealous.

31. Don't assume you know how someone else feels (AKA don't think you can read <u>their</u> minds).

You may know someone well. You may have been in a situation similar to theirs. You may think you know how you would respond even if you HAVEN'T been in their situation. Yet you can't really know how another person feels.

You may decide a friend going through a hard time needs some space because that's what you would want. But they may just need a friend to sit with them or watch a movie or have a coffee.

Just because you'd be upset by something, don't assume your friend is upset and become defensive ahead of time.

Sometimes we project our own emotions onto someone else and respond to something that isn't even there, something false that's all in our heads.

For example, my friend really likes to be taken care of her and have someone sit with her when she's sick. However that friend's husband wants to close the door and be left alone completely when he's sick.

She (incorrectly) assumed when they were first married that it would be a great way to show how much she loved her sick husband to hover around him with chicken soup, offer to watch a movie with him, fuss over his temperature, bring him tea on an hourly basis, and basically do everything she would want in that situation. Yeah. That was a learning experience for both of them. And imagine if her husband had done the reverse without knowing his wife actually wanted all that attention. While their way made sense in each of their minds, it wasn't the way their spouse really wanted to be treated.

That's an example of a concrete action, but it illustrates the point: that others will (again!) view things differently than you and you can't assume you know what that looks like unless you ask.

32.   It's not all about you.

Don't worry so much about what other people think. Honestly.

I have spent years trying to impress everyone around me. Working hard, trying to fit in. But I've found an important truth: it's not really working. People you're (and I'm) trying to impress most likely aren't going to notice.

To be honest, they're not even thinking about you. They're focused on themselves, what YOU think of THEM, and their own insecurities.

Also under this topic: not everything that's hurt you was designed to be hurtful. Distractedness, busy-ness, ignorance, general cluelessness can be the source of someone's hurtful action, or inaction, rather than a desire to cause you pain.

can think of many times I dropped the ball or thoughtlessly said something lame that probably really hurt someone and damaged the relationship I had with them. It wasn't out of a motive to hurt, it just slipped by.

33. Motives.

Look carefully a person's motives rather than their actions or words alone.

Here's what I mean. If someone who really cares about you is doing something (or saying something) that's hard or painful for you, look to see where their heart is. Are they looking out for their best interest or yours? What is motivating them to address the topic with you? Are they doing it from a place of love? Whether you agree with what their saying or not, try to see what's behind their words or actions.

A good friend once took the time to bring up a very hard topic with me. I didn't want to hear it and part of me just wanted to get up and walk away from the conversation, but I could see a heart of great concern within her, a heart that truly wanted the best for me. So I listened. I may not have agreed, but I heard her out and understood she loved me enough to share this difficult thing.

This cuts both ways. If there's someone who's overly agreeable and all about complementing you, look at their motives. Try to see what they may want from you and what they may be trying to gain by building a relationship. Some people are, sadly, out for what they can get and don't have your best interest at heart. Their motives for associating with you may not be the purest.

And another way to look at this topic: examine YOUR motives. Before you launch into something, ask yourself what you're trying to gain by these words/actions/relationships. Is it for your own benefit, for the joy of getting even (which rarely works out well), or for the other person's best interest?

We all have the "why" behind the "what" in our words and actions. Seeking out the "why" can give a much clearer view of the situation than looking only at the "what."

34. Don't judge where you haven't walked.

It's human nature to make snap judgements about people or situations based on what we see on the surface of things or what things appear to be in the moment. But these judgements are rarely fair, accurate, or helpful.

Time and again this has proven true for me. I look at a person or situation, decide based on my limited perspective what's going on, and make a call on how I will react to said person or situation. Without knowing.

We can only see what is presented right in front of us, but when the curtain is pulled back, things can look altogether different.

We can judge another person's anger or rudeness without knowing or understanding their pain. We can judge the way a situation is handled without knowing all the intricacies of how things really are. We haven't walked the path, so we REALLY don't know how we would respond in the same place. And we can't know.

So we need to choose (there's that word again) to give the benefit of the doubt, to reserve judgement, and to love. Even if the person isn't especially lovable at the moment.

Love the person, reserve judgement on what you can't know.

35. Decide what really does and doesn't matter.

I said this earlier, but it bears repeating. Perfection is an illusion at best and a toxic lie at worst. It's a standard we strive for that no one ever reaches. No one. Ever.

The sooner you understand that, the better. That doesn't mean you don't work for excellence in what you do, using your unique blend of talents, gifts, and passions, but it does mean you can't compare yourself with the Facebook-Pinterest-Instagram-filtered world you see on a screen.

For years, before any of those media were on the scene, I constantly compared what I did, what I looked like, what my house looked like with what I saw in magazines or on HGTV. And I always came up short.

In the sum of it all, people never remember if your home is perfect or if the silverware matched. They don't remember whether your nails were done or if your outfit was the latest trend or the best label. They remember how you made them feel. That you took the time to sit and talk with them, to make a cup of tea for them, to fix a meal and share an evening.

When you're stressing about something- anything!- ask yourself: Will this matter in 5 minutes? In 5 hours? In 5 weeks? In 5 years?

Decide what is most important to you. Act on the important things. And don't stress about the small things.

36. In closing.

You are one-of-a-kind, custom made for the life you are meant to have. Not another person in human history has your perfect potpourri of talents, strengths, passions, beauty, flaws, and fears. You are unique and have incredible things within you and ahead of you. Never forget that. You have great purpose in this world and can affect great change for good.

And you're really extra special to me since you read all the way to the end of my book. My deepest hope is that some of what I shared strikes a chord, if not today, then it will resound when life hands you a circumstance that reminds you of one of these glances in my rear view mirror.

As I wrote this, I thought of my daughter, standing tip-toe on the edge of adulthood, and myself at that time in my life. I imagined what I would want to say to my long-ago self, what I would say to my daughter today.   And I thought of the young, wonderful, potential-filled women who might read my words, and all they have to offer this world. So go. Offer it.

Follow the passion in your heart- do what you love, and love what you do.

Don't settle for a life half-lived- look for the beauty in every hard circumstance.

Be the very best version of who you are.

Rejection is better than regret- take that step that scares you as long as it leads toward the dream you carry in your deepest heart.

Be your own original, exceptional, inimitable, singular kind of amazing.

CPSIA information can be obtained
at www.ICGtesting.com
Printed in the USA
LVOW05s0336030616
491074LV00026B/368/P